Balls for a One-Armed Juggler

IRVING LAYTON

IRVING LAYTON

Balls for a One-Armed Juggler

MCCLELLAND AND STEWART LIMITED

DESIGN: *Frank Newfeld*

The Canadian Publishers
McClelland & Stewart Limited
25 Hollinger Road/Toronto 16

Contents

FOR AVIVA

Balls for a One-Armed Juggler

There was once a one-armed juggler

who had two eyes, two ears, two feet,

and two huge balls which he tossed into

the air and called the antinomies ...

●

•

Foreword

Today, poets must teach themselves to imagine the worst. To apprehend the enormity of the filth, irrationality, and evil that washes in on us from the four corners of the earth, they must have the severity to descend from one level of foulness to another and learn what the greatest of them had always known: there is, of course, no bottom, no end. Because he has not done this the modern poet has been contemptuously pushed aside by novelists, playwrights, and film-makers looking for the terrible meanings imbedded in the human ash of death factories. Where, then, have the poets been? Where are they now? Asleep? No, they are not asleep; they are still muttering their favourite incantations before nature, death, love, pleased if someone overhears them and recommends them for a travelling fellowship or a university post. Most of them are unaware that their excellent lines hopping with half-rhyme, slant rhyme, and internal rhyme, have become delicious archaisms. What a great to-do was made, just yesterday, about trimming poetry down and making it indistinguishable from good speech. But what exactly do you propose talking about? What are you going to become conversational, informal, and passionate about? Usury? Sex? Anglicanism? Limestone? Interesting topics, certainly, but hardly to the point in an age of mass terror, mass degradation, when the human being has less value than a bedbug or a cockroach.

What insight does the modern poet give us into the absolute evil of our times? Where is the poet who can make clear for us Belsen? Vorkuta? Hiroshima? The utter wickedness of Nazism and National-Communism? There is no poet in the English-speaking world who gives me the feeling that into his lines have entered the misery and crucifixion of our age. His psychology, pre-Freudian; his political thought, pre-totalitarian; his metaphysics, non-existent, his well-meant blabbings originate in a bourgeois-Christian humanism

•

totally unable to account for the vilenesses enacted by men and women of this century. Does the aestheticism of Pound explain them? The sweatless paganism of Wallace Stevens? Innocency, naïveté, the decencies and dullnesses of the clergyman. Nowhere is the image of man portrayed that might have stiffened us for the cruelty, perversion, systematic lying, and monstrous hypocrisy of the totalitarian regimes of Hitler's Germany and Stalin's Russia, or the no less damnable perversions and hypocrisies of the European bourgeois and imperialist. When I say nowhere, I mean nowhere in poetry. Turn to the novel or the play, and the frightful hideousness of contemporary man is their constant theme and preoccupation. Man, without a soul; man, robotized; man, tortured, humiliated, and crucified; man, driven into slave camps and death factories by devils and perverts; man, the dirtiest predator of all. The novelists: Kafka, Dostoievsky, Lawrence, Faulkner; the playwrights: Beckett, Genet, Ionescu—almost every page of theirs is a condemnation and a warning. The poets? Pound's mid-Western blat about Social Credit? Eliot's weary Anglicanism? Yeats's fairytale Byzantium? In these vicious, revolutionary times? Don't make me laugh. Frost's jaunty pastoralism? Auden's sensationalistic mishmash of psychoanalysis, Marxism, and Christianity? What a sour, boring joke!

With only a few exceptions—Lawrence, Rimbaud—the modern poet has been an empty windbag and a chatterer. No wonder anguished people turn from him in amusement, boredom, or pity. He has nothing to say worth listening to. One asks for bread and is given a plethora of sounds. The major poets are children lost in a painted forest, making as much noise as they can to attract attention; the lesser ones absent-mindedly continue bringing their posies into the swept courtyards of Auschwitz and Belsen; all of them intent on proving to the world how sensitive they are, how perceptive, how erudite and archetype-crammed. The truth is this: instead of remembering they are prophets and the descendants of prophets, the poets have swapped roles with entertainers and culture-peddlers.

•

They have refused the crown of thorns. Because he is a prophet, the poet must take into himself all the moral diseases, all the anguish and terror of his age, so that from them he can forge the wisdom his tortured fellowmen need to resist the forces dragging them down into the inhuman and the bestial. No doubt it is more pleasant for the contemporary poet to put that cup aside or hand it on to others; more pleasant to regard himself as a surrogate for the displaced clergyman or priest, breathing spasmodically before the True, the Good, and the Beautiful. Or even to think of himself as a picturesque rebel or a colourful bohemian who livens up the parties of jaded suburbanites, or as a scholar and wit. More pleasant; also more applaudable by university presidents, literary scribes, and culture-philistines. But the penalty for this fiddle-faddling is the seepage of life out of his poetry. The age has left him behind, and the best he can give us today are consolatory beautiful mouthings and clever semantic riddles to provide profitable employment for hordes of English profs.

What must concern the artist today, above all, is the organized nature of twentieth-century wickedness. Certainly this wickedness builds on evil that has existed in human beings from earliest beginnings; but present-day pressures have created a type of *massenmensch*—homeless, estranged, degraded—to whom violence and cruelty offer the only relief from his nagging feelings of resentment and inferiority. He has no use for a culture that excludes him and that he feels rests upon a lie. For the historians, poets, analysts, and other apologists of this lie he has a limitless, unsleeping contempt. When he runs into one of these sippers of culture-consommé he wants nothing so much as to break a bottle over his head—not to teach him good sense or a respect for truth—but because he's pushed by obscure impulses no one has troubled to explain to him or wanted to exorcise. Perhaps they can never be exorcised. Perhaps the alienated, murderous individual is the unavoidable product of our runaway technologism and naïve scientism. By atomizing society into isolated units, into masses and mobs without

•

roots or ties, they have turned the professional man no less than the plumber and electrician into unfeeling, inarticulate barbarians.

Surely the first thing to note is the exceptionally heinous nature of twentieth-century evil. Things have been done to human beings by other human beings for which no other century or epoch can offer any parallel. Beside the mass slaughters, crimes, cynical treacheries, perversions, and unheard-of cruelties of the Nazis and Bolsheviks, the carnage and razings commanded by an Attila or Crassus appear relatively mild, decorous affairs—normal human wickedness. It was left for this century to produce two monsters without their peer in the history of mankind: Hitler and Stalin. Only in this century has the distinction between guilty and innocent been systematically wiped out, masses of people been put to death for abstract, ideological reasons, and deceit and terror employed on so immense a scale to reduce whole populations to terrified helots. There is a frightful stink in the souls of all men and women living today. Auschwitz, Hiroshima, Vorkuta, the Soviet frame-up trials of the 'thirties: with these man touched the infiniteness of evil—and survived! The stink in his soul is not only that of burning flesh, of decomposing bones. It is also the stink of self-guilt. At last he knows the truth about himself and of what he's capable. Nevertheless, so perverse is the human being, he cannot but be pleased with the outcome, even with the entire titanic drama that made possible his unique distinction. More than anyone before him, twentieth-century man had extended his being into the realm of evil; and though he looks fearfully at the remaining moral scars, he does not do so without a certain dark pride and exultation. The Luciferian ambition and delight: anything, as long as one is first!

If the poet is to win back the praise he once enjoyed as the supreme "interpreter of his age" he must learn again to address himself to the moral and psychological dilemmas of his time. Though satisfying verbally and technically, mere blabbermouthing is out. He must shake himself free from the professors; indeed, from the bulk

•

of his present-day admirers. There is a new, dark knowledge waiting to be assimilated into the minds and consciences of those who are his contemporaries. To make this self-awareness available to them, the poet will have to crawl out of the universities and academies to roam the streets and alleyways of the megalopoli. He will have to stop watching for approving signals from pedants and book-loving critics. In silent anguish he will absorb the evil of his times, himself place the crown of thorns on his head. He needs no other adornment. Forging ever subtler tools, he cannot permit himself to forget he addresses mankind at large, not small coteries of the sensitive and frightened. He will impatiently dismiss the limiting conventions of the so-called fathers of modern poetry (Eliot, Pound, Yeats) or any exhortation that would keep him from dealing with the seminal conflicts of the age in which he lives. If he doesn't there are others who will. There are the novelists and playwrights to whom he has already surrendered much. Should the poet forget his prophetic role he will continue to be applauded by culture-philistines and commissars and by all who fear to hear the truth spoken boldly and imaginatively, but as a voice calling for human dignity and worth, for charity, freedom, and sacrifice, he will have ceased to exist.

Montreal, Quebec
September 11, 1962

·

There Were No Signs

By walking I found out
where I was going.

By intensely hating, how to love.
By loving, whom and what to love.

By grieving, how to laugh from the belly.

Out of infirmity, I have built strength.
Out of untruth, truth.
From hypocrisy, I weaved directness.

Almost now I know who I am.
Almost I have the boldness to be that man.

Another step
And I shall be where I started from.

•

For Aviva, Because I Love Her

I saw a spider eating a huge bee.

First he ate my limbs;
and then he removed my head, feasting
   on the quivering jellies of my eyes
and on what passes among bees for ears.

And though dead,
I could feel, with each morsel he had,
that he enjoyed his repast
   and I was glad.

Afterwards he sliced me down the middle,
exposing my insides
   to the burning mid-day heat;
and slowly the voluptuous spider
feasted on my jewelled organs,
abolishing them one by one,
till I was all gone, all swallowed up,
   except for my love of you:

My radiant wings—these, ah, these
he did not touch
but left glinting in the sun.

•

Silence

For Ernest Hemingway

The word betrays the act;
The act alone is pure.
The rest is literature:
Fishbait for fools and pedants.

Look at that mountain back,
Knife-edge poised against the sky.
A single bird flies over it
And disappears.

At that height nothing dies;
All is unyielding, eternal.
And I imagine the cries
Of the unsacrificed birds.

I imagine the only music
I hear—soundless, unchangeable.
I am in love with silence,
With the hardness of silence.

I shall become
Like that stone
Through whose single cleft
Flows the stillest water.

•

The Imbecile

By mistake I came to White Mountain Lodge,
Thinking it was an inn. I asked for beer,
And the thin man who opened the door grinned:
"It happens almost each day; people think
This damned place an enchanting public-house
But it isn't . . ." He peered to make certain
No one would overhear him. "It's for boys
Who . . ." and made a sign I took in at once.
And, appearing moved, I said: "Cretins, eh?
The feeble-minded? Or perhaps the sins
Of the too rich?" I could see my bluntness
Displeased, and he believed me God-knows-what.
"Yes, that's what they are," he nodded.
                              "They work?"
I then asked. Behind me were small hillocks
And untouched fields that could be put to use.
"Why don't they raise onions, leeks, flowers?"
The man now smiled. "These boys are fortunate;
They don't have to, having sires with wealth."
I saw his careful frown as I flung back:
"But what of those who chose penniless sires?

●

Or would no one here be such an idiot?"
And, laughing, went off warmed by my own wit
To run straight into a small slackjawed boy
With eyes that were vacant. A net of froth
Hung from his thickened lips. "Hi, chief," he called
As a slouching dog—pure mongrel—approached
From behind to bark and worry my boots,
Though with an undertone of fear, I thought.
The idiot boy shushed him into silence.
"Chucky's like that since a bad old truck
Knocked him down . . . an' . . . an' he almost died . . .
His skin was all torn up n' everything . . ."
He bent down and held the dog. "Poor doggie . . ."
O inextinguishable spark of love!
I marvelled at the imbecile's pity
Welling up through the slime that hid his lips
And the blank eyes that held the world's dumb grief
Like panes made clean for a single image.
And my own were wet for him, this cockeyed world
That makes disasters for the human heart,
And myself shamed by this cretinous boy.

Elegy for Marilyn Monroe

Last summer, it was "Papa" Hemingway
This summer it's Marilyn Monroe
Next summer, who?—Who will it be?
But Orville Faubus gets re-elected
Two hundred million X-Laxed Americans
   go on defecating as before
and Congress acts as if nothing has happened.
How come I asked of Lyndon Johnson
   there's no Committee
to investigate
the high rate of suicide
among those with a tragic overplus
of sensitivity and consciousness;
and received a postcard
   showing a Texan oil field.

Gentlemen, take it for what it's worth
but I suspect something more terrible
   than radioactive fallout
or the unmentionable gases of Belsen
has penetrated our human atmosphere.
The PTA's haven't heard of it yet
or the Board Directors of Bell Tel
or President Kennedy;
moreover if I manoeuvred to let them know
   what it is
there'd be a Congressional committee
to investigate me!
They'd get cracking at once. O yes.

●

You ask, what is it
that goes straight for its victims like radar?
I name it the Zed-factor,
lethal only to the passionate, the imaginative,
    and to whatever is rare and delightful
in this brute universe.
Invisible as halitosis or body odour
it makes no warning of its presence;
therefore no TV outfit
will sing commercials to it
with chuckling hooligans
    poking fingers through plugged drains,
and anyhow since only an infinitesimal part
of the nation
is susceptible to attack
why bother? See, why bother?

Good-bye Marilyn
It's raining in Magog
    a town you probably never heard of
where I sit in a tavern writing this;
nor did you ever hear of me
though I once composed a whole poem to you
and called you "Earth Goddess."
The janitors to whom you said hello,
the cabbies who spotted you by your stride
    and magnificent blonde hair
and whistled and honked their horns
to let you know their good luck,

●

the men all around the world
who touched your limbs in irreverent sleep
will miss your wiggle and crazy laugh,
but no one more than I
dazed this afternoon by grief and drink;
for I loved you from the first
who know what they do not know,
seeing in your death a tragic portent
for all of us who crawl and die
under the wheeling, disappearing stars;
and who must now live with the self-complacent,
    the enduring dull,
without your sustaining radiance,
your rarity.

From here on in
they have it, the pygmies have it,
it's all theirs!

Good-bye Marilyn
Sleep, sleep peacefully tonight
One poet at least will remember
    your brightness,
the unique fever in your form and face
(O insuperable filament, now black, now ash!)
and love you always.

●

Still Life

We were speaking of modern art.

"The human's no longer interesting,"
said the stranger.
"God, nature, man,
we've exhausted them each in turn."

It was a warm August afternoon,
and the linnet kept wiping its beak
on the fallen leaves and grass,
joyfully ignoring both of us.

As if he had done this
many times before,
the stranger dislodged the flat stone
near his hand
and let it crash down heavily
on the hopping bird.

Only the fluttering wing was visible,
and it looked
as if the ridiculous stone
was attempting to fly.

Then stillness: stone on wing: both partially
in shadow.
There was a sweet smell of earth.

"That makes an exciting composition,"
observed the stranger.

•

The Well-Wrought Urn

"What would you do
if I suddenly died?"

"Write a poem to you."

"Would you mourn for me?"

"Certainly," I sighed.

"For a long time?"

"That depends."

"On what?"

"The poem's excellence," I replied.

For Alexander Trocchi, Novelist

And you, Alexander Trocchi,
high on the high seas,
innocent Christ on the lam,
charged fugitive:
as the blue waves surged across the deck
did you believe them constabulary
flashing their sudden badges
to nab you before you could jab
the Father's peace into your veins?
And when the sky ejaculated stars
over its solitary pitching bed
did you hold the captains at bay?
At nervous needlepoint compel
the ship toward listless harbours
where tropical purple waves
lift forever their enchanting poppies?
Did you finally run
smack into the arm of the Almighty,
and was his arm scarred too?
I hope, Trocchi, before you die
the ancestral monkey on your back
will switch into the Most High;
give you his convulsed vein
to jab it full of heroin
and letting you lead his penitent hand
across your pocked and exiled face,
indite for each scared Jack of us
a truer version of Creation
—your first masterpiece.

•

No Wild Dog

I tell my class
What man can do
No cobra can
And no wild dog

Or other kinds
Of vicious beast:
The prowling wolf
And the mongoose.

I'm told they hate
The smell of gas
And run from fires;
But that's not it

No, that's not it.
It takes reason
And spirit too
Which man alone

Evolved in time
So he can do
The amazing things
No cobra can

And no wild dog.

•

Androgyne

Were Death a woman I should never die.
So jealous is my loving wife that I
Could look upon a passing hearse and sneer
At this dumb show of frail mortality.
For what from Death would I have then to fear

Who might not even by her darkest guile,
Her frowned commands, her most sensual smile,
Tear me from my Love? Tell me, who'd encroach
On her whose fingers stiffen to a file,
Seeing a woman from afar approach?

No, certainly I shall live forever;
For my dear wife will be immortal too
As one whom Death, androgynous lover,
Rages against my jealousy to woo.
Only by dread compact shall we be free
For waiting Death to ravish her and me.

The Cage

I turn away to hide my terror
Lest my unmanliness displease them
And maim for all a half-holiday
Begun so well, so auspiciously.
They are building the mythical cage
Whose slow rise allows janitors, whores,
And bank presidents to display love
To one another like a curious
Wound: the Elect to undertake feats
Of unusual virtue. Masons
Give stone and ironmongers, metal
As if these were forever useless
In a paradise of leaves and sun;
And a blacksmith, handsome and selfless,
Offers to blind me at once without
Charge. A quiet shiver of self-love,
Of self-approbation runs through each
At the discovery of so much
Altruism—unknown, hitherto,
Unsuspected—in their very midst.
The instance of the meek stonemasons,
The ironmongers and the selfless blacksmith
Seizes like a panic. Suddenly
Each one vies with his neighbour, avid
To seek out the more burdensome toil:
This one lugging spikes; that one, planks.
Affecting it is to watch their grace,
Their fine courtesies to each other
When they collide; or to imagine
Their tenderness in bed when they leave
The square littered with balloons and me
Blinded and raging in this huge cage.

•

Therapy

When I was six
our cat littered behind the stove:
four kittens sound in mind and limb
and one lame.

The lame one
had all my love
—dragging its sick leg
in chase with the others,
all my agonized attention.

It was its playfulness
with a ball
broke my heart at last;
and I was glad
to see the kitten lying, one afternoon,
deadstill
when I returned from school.

Yesterday
for the first time in my life
I axed a young badger
rummaging in our garbage bin
for food.

And though he wobbled
a short distance
before he keeled over,
I am now strong enough for God and Man.

•

No Shish Kebab

Mayakovsky had it.
Cafavy.
And Tuvim, the Jewish Pole.

Byron also: probably
the only English poet
who did, not forgetting
you know who.
(Form mistress, Miss Snell,
is nescient
of her hero's Greek bum boy
but knows the leaves
of his thirty-sixth year
were all brown and sere.)

Keats and Shelley didn't.
And not, definitely, Milton.
John Donne?
A smidgen, perhaps; no more.
And in his youth only.

Caught lifting it
from the decadent French,
Thomas Stearns Eliot
resolved to go straight
into the Anglican Church, and did;
nevertheless, the pew he sat in
was redolent
of spiced meats only.
Pray for him now
and at the cocktail hour.

•

And Maude Gonne
gave Willie Yeats
a smell of it;
and later, old age.
In between
he was a charlatan,
a flaneur
pretending to smell it
when of course
he didn't, not really.

Can it be
the nullibicity of its odour,
warm and corrupt,
is what makes
certain anal professors
of English Lit.
stare all day at mirrors,
and their wives at inkblots
for the manifestations
of genius?

That must be it!
What else?

·

Political Economy

My son, said the repellent old man,
make certain you never need do
the dirty work of civilization.

All political credos, all religions
are necessary persuasions
to get the poor beggars into the mines.

That a few be whole, many must be broken.
All reform rests on hypocrisy:
fringe benefits for slaves and menials.

Fixed and eternal is the law of gravity:
so, my son, are injustice and the class war.
Living is an affair for aristocrats.

•

The Ritual Cut

At Paperman's Funeral Home,
noting my tremulous mouth,
the pious attendant
slit my tie
—a ritual cut.

Then for his service
held up his hand,
the dry palm towards me.

Truly ours is a creed
for the living,
not for the dead
in their pocketless shrouds.

And anyway it wasn't his mother
was going to be buried
that grey morning.

•

Mashed Potatoes

I walked into a packed restaurant.

I saw hundreds
of unimportant faces
working themselves into a fever of excitement.

Near the door
a repressed nine-to-five slave
green with matrimony
was adjusting his collar.

I asked him:
What about biography?
Has it a future?

He pointed to the cashier
who opened her mouth wide
and yawned: her lower jaw
was a stadium of culture-centres.

•

Over the remains of a calf's liver
a starry-eyed couple
was talking of love
and naming their prospective infants.

Skol! Abi gezunt!

I reached the bus terminal
at the stroke of seven.

Commuters pressed against me
as if my good looks were contagious,
and I had a sudden vision
of mashed potatoes.

But these had their coats on.

●

Not in Vain

She showed me her child's birth certificate:
  Baptême dans le nom de Dieu

She an immigrant, poor, friendless, alone.

O yes, they had taken her infant.
O yes, they had paid all her lying-in expenses.
O yes, he was probably well on the way
  to becoming a priest.

What was she doing now?

She was looking after the two children
  of a rich manufacturer of crucifixes
  separated from his indolent, man-loving bitch.

And I was made proud by the knowledge
  that in this province at least, it was plain
  the thralls of the Church were so ardent and pitiful
no little bastard was ever going to grow up
to take the name of his Lord in vain.

Homo Oeconomicus

for Nikita

A whole society was reared
On Marx's carbuncles and beard;
The repressions of Herr Hegel
Interfuse the General Will
That seeks for each more liberty
By forcing all men to be free
And makes the heretic a foe.
His best disciple was Rousseau.
The poet's visions or the saint's,
The mad ecstacies mystics paint;
Erasmus, Spinoza, the best
Of Leveller and Anabaptist
Have all by strange ways led to this:
A heaven of consumers' bliss
Where never the seed of Adam
Shall cry for conscience or freedom
But huge coupons to get and spend
On products produced without end,
Their one god reverenced truly
The insatiable belly
And their most radiant vision
A supermarket on the moon.
From everywhere comes up the stench
Of technology's *massenmensch*;
Not a man really, but a tool.
Frightened, alienated, dull;
A machine part, replaceable
Or thrown away as scrap; a null
Without brain, perplexity, heart,
Without philosophy or art.

•

The incitements of a great love?
What! Are you mad? In a bee-hive!
At the behest of the good State
Like insects he and his kind mate,
Their induced delights useful for
Enlarging the labour force or
Adding another voiceless shout
When a Leader is in or out.
O world where the chiefest concern
Of commissar, physician
Is to stock the proper drugs, smiles,
To prevent either cramps or piles!
Where zombies read their bulletin
And dispense with holiness, sin;
Where Mind's replaced by the Vozhd's speech,
The barked command, the radio's screech;
Or the rebel's prophetic wrath
By smile & nod of bureaucrat;
And that which true men once named Art,
By some Ukrainian's burp or fart.

•

History as a Slice of Ham

The Gks: they took stock of many gods.

The Hebes, out by only one,
suffered macerations and death,
being closest to the truth. Ah, Jesu,
jewboy worshipped in cloisters:
abhorring oysters and swinemeat,
they offended their gentle neighbours.

An odd people, greatly mad.
I, sprung from their loins,
and reverencing neither Dieu nor Gott,
only Eros in my body's temple
see my grandsire's bloodstained face
expiring in the slice of ham, ha! ha!
I daily relish and eat.

●

Sören Kierkegaard

He sees your humped back and calls you cripple.
Your walk, your talk, offend this philistine;
This, this less than philistine, this Noman
Who devotedly will whore and tipple,
And maim should Christian rulers tell him to
Nipponese and Negro, Ukrainian, Jew.

Ah, he's a fine fellow who calls you cripple;
Whose mind, whose appetites are razor-keen.
Culture-lover, sportsman, philanthropist,
His linen and his mistresses always clean:
But hating you because you had not missed
The deformity no one else had seen.

Change

We were looking at the October landscape.

I turned to my friend,
an excellent man, a revolutionary,
but totally lacking in imagination:

"What, did you once tell me,
was the true complexion
of Fidel's communism?"
And feigning to have forgotten,
I stammered: "Olive? . . . Brown? . . . Vermilion?"
and saw him turn a shade green.

He pointed to the hillside.
"All right, so Castro evolved! Even
the trees are turning Communist," he sneered.

I stroked my beard
and looked past him.
"But they never stay that way," I replied.

•

This Machine Age

For fifteen cents
the label read,
the Virgin's halo
would light up
for three minutes.
The man dropped
the pieces of money
into the machine's slot
and looked about
the vast, gloomy church
empty except
for him and me.
When his gaze came back
to the halo
it was still unlit
—a dark infuriating zero.

•

He gave the machine
a careful kick
to bring the lights
of the circle out.
It didn't.
"Damn it!" he shouted,
"Why doesn't it light up?"
He kicked again
and muttered something
I didn't hear.
But I could guess
from the way he looked
he thought divine sereneness
a poker-faced fraud
and himself taken in
by the Mother of God.

·

Neighbour Love

A grove
of tall unoffending trees
separates our cottages

Bang! Bang!

Jesus! how can I love my neighbour
when each morning, hour after hour,
even before the first bird has cheeped
he's out driving nails into boards and plinths?

What a racket!
Excusable only if he's building
his own coffin, a six-foot bungalow
by the placid lake

May the hammer fly from his hand,
his body suddenly shrivel
and a crazy carpenter hack off his tool
to use as a plug for a small knothole

Or let him live to be old as Nestor
and the hideous noise he makes
without let-up ring in his ears
but amplified a thousand thousandfold

No, may his next-door neighbour
drive a long shining nail into his skull
so that I can compose verses
and love my neighbour again.

A Grotesque Pair

M. Sartre and Simone de Beauvoir,
What a grotesque, amusing, silly pair!
He fools himself as a clever man does
By finding wit in every verbal fuzz;
She thinks it one of Nature's dirty tricks
To have devised the loathsome female sex;
He rages at the going of teeth, hair
And calls it Existentialist despair
(Ho! he's a wise man who tells us plainly
The world's absurd if flesh is born to die.)
She protests she writes, fights, does all one can,
And yet never quite makes it as a man.
Both rave, rant, storm, write books & articles
Because it's each other they do not please:
How can the universe make any sense
If they're dismissed by French intelligence—
Each other's! Their amour-propre so hurt,
They dart & hop like two birds, bright, alert,
Yet somehow empty—and quite bodiless:
Have they not looked into each other's eyes?

•

The Real Values

Rabbi, why do you move heaven and earth
to blow breath
into this lifeless body,
drowned under the surfeit
of Chinese food and pizzapie?

The good life destroyed him:
distilleries, supermarkets.
Long ago he packed away his soul
in the clothing industry.

Examine the hideous, putrefying face,
the fishy eyes
and gross mouth, open
as though to swallow
another cooked lentil.

Isaiah, hop to it, Moses—
bring on the condiments, the plum sauce!

•

Your noble gas
about Torah, Halachah
affords a passing tingle
to worshippers breathless with emulation,
especially to wives and daughters
musing on fabled hairdos.

Save your breath, rabbi.
No, save your money.

And learn from your bloated flock
bored by whisky and wifeswapping,
the burnt offerings on Sunday,
how to invest sensibly
in real estate values.

So that you can speak the truth
as I do.

•

Drunk on McGill Campus
for Sabine

My veins are full of alcohol
I lie sprawled on the grass
The sun warms my face
And warms my bare chest

A lovely redhead
Plops a live sparrow
Into her mouth
I'm the hub: the world wheels about

And the grey buildings
Begin to shake and dance
Books tumble out of library windows
And burst into pure joy

While a lone Nubian
Shoots up taller than a tree
He's the sun's ambassador
My credentials, Sir—a hiccup!

•

He moves with slow dignity
Smiling like a prince
And draws his train of shadow
From the lowest branches

Over the restless buttocks
Of the fig-leaved statues
The campus fountain throws
Its cold sunspangled spray

Like a drunken lover
I pull down the sky
To kiss: and there where my lips touch
Appears a joyous white star.

•

On Rereading the Beats

If only it were *that* easy to write poems

Look at me, I'm standing on my head
Look at me, I'm whacking my doodle
Look at me, I'm making paste out of earwax
Look at me, I'm pissing into a flowerpot:
   the steam rises and hisses, "Saint-Saens"

O if it were that easy

To take American brag, American ignorance, American
vulgarity, American provincialism & superficiality,
American prevarication & hucksterism, and watch them
expand & expand like a non-illuminating gas till they
filled up the largest warehouse in San Francisco or the
biggest emporium in Chicago; and then to paste a label
on the forehead of the building in large block letters
for everyone from the President down to see:

     POETRY   ADMISSION FREE

If poetry cd. forget its origin in song & metaphor; cd.
forget it was genuine like Alp snow or childbirth; cd.
be sold over the counter like olives/booze; held up
like a stagecoach in a phoney Wild West and made to stand
& deliver; or become the nation's official con game like
Italian Enalotto or our own Bingo before the cops stepped in
and scattered it to the outlying paroisses.

De Tocqueville, you are justified
De Tocqueville, you are vindicated
De Tocqueville, you were dead right

•

From the debased amorphous mobs pouring out
of the American megalopoli like exhaust fumes
blackening kiosks & storefronts what else but:
megalomania, narcissism, hysteria, effeminacy,
coarseness, ignobility, and the mindless iteration
about LOVE ad nauseam
                                        Faugh!
And COMRADESHIP and BROTHERHOOD

O these swine that need collective showers for cleansing!

They almost make me prefer
    the Eton boys & eunuchs of England
—almost I said almost
At least the Beats have vitality!
Yet vitality proves nothing except that something is alive
So is a polecat; so is a water-rat
Excitation is not excitement; and energy is fine, boys,
but who admires the energy of a self-flagellant or sadist?
Consider the animation of a garbage heap in mid-August: its
    seethe & flow of maggots; you may never hope to equal that,
and be advised the frenzy of a trapped bluebottle is not poetic
Moreover you ought to be ashamed to hide between the flowing
    robes of Plato & Buddha
    with evil-smelling dung on your fingers
If you must retch at the sight of your smeared fingers
    do so decently, in privacy & in your own sinks
Above everything, do not hold a pen with them and write about
    your lovely desires. No one will believe you,
least of all your comrades
    who will measure and know you, quite naturally,
by their own feculent selves.

The Disguise

"Composed is the world of unfeeling swine,"
Declared the grey-haired and gentle stranger,
"And what blooms best here are barren hearts
Where fools need potions for sex and hunger.
Men do not love as once their fathers loved:
Their neighbour's suffering leaves them all unmoved.

"Compassionless as stone they have their day,
Forgetful that love's increase, the Ideal
Is man's sole meaning and his hallowed way."
Behind his words' merit why did I feel
The cruel intent and the guarded insult
In so hoisting love against our common fault?

•

Thanatos

I'd rather you didn't mention him.
If you've any thoughts on the subject
Let them lie blackening on your brain
Where after a fiasco, some slugs
Of gin, a meditative stanza
Will shape itself like a cypress leaf.
Give him the silent treatment; I say,
Pay him in his own dull coin. Talking
Of him is what he wants most, and scares
The poor old folks hearing his name dropped.
To hell with grave subjects; a plague fall
On poets who have tragic visions
When their members like Dali clockhands
Soften on vague sundials of hair.
Cart them away, I say; and give me
That other vision, the comic one;
And mad laughter blowing out of cleft
Of breasts and buttocks—Cleopatra's,
Of course! I'm subtle, man, O subtle
And no mother's milk behind my ears:
And can, yes, croak with the best of them;
Have too, in my time, from a windy
Nook, and been provocative and deep
And coupled him with Sex, with Love,
And bawled and raged at the failing light
That hid a wet pussy from my eyes.
But I've an amorous tongue between
My teeth, and hands to feel with, haven't I?
And if croaking is your great grand theme,
The frogs can do that so much better
At the pond's drear edge when the sun leaves
And the shades lie thick upon their backs.

•

The Pillar

Using the moist end
of a half-smoked cigar
and afterwards,
for apter demonstration,
a white pillar
in the crumbling graveyard,
I taught my darling
how to provoke love.

Now she cannot look
at a funeral wreath
or see a hearse
go past
without her pants
wetting.

•

Mixed Metaphors

I love your poems, she said,
And kept stroking my thighs;
I love their intense thrust
And their hatred of lies.

I spend whole nights with them
—Your book's beside my bed;
For hour on hour I try
To keep them in my head.

I never felt the joys
Of poetry before,
Yet now I mean to know
Them more and more and more!

Your poems are lovely things:
So strong, yet sensitive;
Were they taken from me,
I would not care to live.

And yet because they're thrust
Into my soul so deep,
You must pluck them from me
That I may have my sleep.

•

Baudelaire in a Summer Cottage

He sports his son's peaked cap;
Thinks, under his wife's prodding,
His dispraise of Baudelaire
Has somehow offended me
And blurts out at suppertime,
His glass of Chablis twinkling,
His blue boyish eyes twinkling:
"You . . . *you're* a fine poet, man;
Superb craftsman. Superb." Looks
Conspiratorially
To his wife for approval
And adjusts his son's peaked cap.
She, intelligent and French,
(Really, need one add to this?)
Who considers me—all men,
The vegetation itself,
A raging impetigo
Covering our sad planet,
Smiles therapeutically

At her husband, pats his hand
While I again grieve over
The future of poetry,
I mean: communication
Passionate and unrehearsed
Between warm men and women;
Seeing the cancer spreading fast,
Destroying self-expression,
Destroying uniqueness, force,
And that which makes intercourse
Between humans sweet and good,
I mean: authenticity.
So I say, "Yes, Baudelaire
Though mad was free as the air
And so's every true poet."
And look at the jerk's burnt face,
Thankful he is not quite dead
Who has one ballock snipped off
And one hanging by a thread.

•

Moral with a Story

Her mother used to tell her
only bad women
had well-developed busts.

When her young breasts
began to grow
she was certain Herr Satan
had marked her for his own
and would grab her from below.

They grew & grew,
and their very size
has made Gretchen bold:
one fine swing of them, she says,
would knock the devil out cold.

•

No Cause for Jealousy

My little one, my darling,
are you jealous of the First Lady?

Feature for feature
she may, possibly, have the handsomer face;
or, as you say, more people
to look after it for her.

But yours is the niftier figure.
By far.
Whenever I see you wagging
your eager doggy behind
I'm on fire to wager anyone
you'd beat Marilyn, Liz,
and Mrs Kennedy:
all four of you
stripped, of course,
to remove advantages
they might have
in clothes, jewellery, and so on.

Have they shoulders like yours?
Thighs and navel?
Why, the splendour of your left breast alone
would make them despair
and run to their men for reassurance.
And your neat triangle of hair:
which of them'd top that?

●

You have the figure, my Sweet,
lithe and small,
of an Artemis
and a disposition far more joyous.

And anyhow
look who *your* husband is!

•

Dining Out

There, spliced to a hose manufacturer,
A dull clod, a poor shit with an estate,
She gives him pinch for pinch and shows her teeth;
Yet if he croaked, choked on a marrowbone,
She'd kick him from her like a dying cur.
Her stiletto heels drumming on his skin,
She'd prick a Star of David for each groan:
Her amorous husband would lick the floor.
Ecstatic pair! Finger on nose aslant,
He tells the world she ruts, she smells with love,
And when she has the flowers jacks him off
—While she keeps smiling to the restaurant.

You poor civilized bastards, go, go home,
And screw yourselves into an affection!

•

Involvement

She was immovably certain
she was suffering
from a mysterious malady
of the spirit: one,
complicated and self-flattering.

Every day for a whole week
she fixed vacant eyes on me
and sent me notes
from her darkened bedroom.

Her smile, conveying depths of mud,
oozed over her lips.
She sighed: "Your felicity
in simply being
is vulgar and impractical:
sentimental, if you want the truth;
and your flustered attentions
do not convince."

For a whole week
she improved my mind greatly,
and I was mad to possess her.
Then on the Sabbath: "I know
what you're suffering from," I said.
"What?"
"Yourself," I replied.
And we both rested.

•

Free Djilas

Friday. Nothing unusual.
  We drop out of the skies
with our picket signs
that read: Free Djilas!

The place: Ottawa.
  The astonished citizens
see us assemble
near the Rideau Canal.

And someone, incredulously:
  What is it?
Who is giving it away?
So I tell him to follow us.

As if sprung from the hot asphalt,
  a line of fierce Ottawans
is marching on the Embassy
for a free Djilas.

●

The Predator

The little fox
was lying in a pool of blood,
having gnawed his way out to freedom.

Or the farmhand,
seeing his puny, unprofitable size
had slugged him after with a rifle butt

And he had crawled
to the country roadside
where I came upon him, his fur dust-covered

Hard to believe
a fox is ever dead, that he isn't
just lying there pretending with eyes shut.

His fame's against
him; one suspects him of anything,
even when there's blood oozing from the shut eyes.

His evident
self-enjoyment is against him also:
no creature so wild and gleeful can ever be done for.

•

But this fox was;
there's no place in the world any more
for free and gallant predators like him.

Eagle, lion,
fox and falcon: their freedom is their death.
Man, animal tamed and tainted, wishes to forget.

He prefers bears
in cages: delights to see them pace
back and forth, swatting their bars despondently.

Yet hates himself,
knowing he's somehow contemptible:
with knives and libraries the dirtiest predator of all.

Ghost of small fox,
hear me, if you're hovering close
and watching this slow red trickle of your blood:

Man sets even
more terrible traps for his own kind.
Be at peace; your gnawed leg will be well-revenged.

●

Crazy Jack

Look out!
I can go off any minute.
My mind's full of radioactive material,
my body of loose atoms;
If you detonated me,
an arm of mine
would level the longest street,
my big toe oxidize a supermarket.
I play with the idea
of putting my head into a department store
and watching it go off from a counter.
The shoppers burst out of the windows;
they're off to another world
—or another sale,
draped in blue flame.
Everyone's a Roman candle;
the mobs of downtown Ville Marie
blaze like post-Xmas tinsel.
What an illumination!

How I'd like to explode
before an astonished world!
What else have I to live for?
Can even De Gaulle
propose anything more heroic?

•

Why I Can't Sleep Nights

From the garden
where I had seen nothing growing,
nothing green,
only stiff, mechanical birds
on fragments of chromium

The host led me into his house,
speaking like someone
who does not care to be heard,
certain his words are true
because they had been spoken

Pipes, cylinders, levers,
were all his furnishings,
while circuits of amazing wires
lit up corner bulbs
when I coughed or sneezed

I felt odourless, without weight,
as if my body
was moving independently
between my host and me
though a mirror on each wall
showed me gross and tall

The floors, I recall, were bare
and glistened like polished steel
reflecting my host's skull,
the skin and flesh not at all

•

There was a white light
behind each socket,
and the shadow his person cast
lay on the floor like a soft carpet

A needle came out of the air
and pierced my blue eyes,
spattering the blood
on the bare, polished floor

"This is what the house was made for,"
said my host
as he took me gently by the arm
and led me back into the garden.

•

For My Friend Who Teaches
Literature

I tell you, William,
there isn't a ghost
of a chance
people will be changed by poems.

Book Club editors
wish to believe otherwise,
Commencement Day orators
and commissars;
but we poets know the facts of the case.
People will remain stupid and deceitful,
their hearts will pump
malice and villainy
into their bloodstream forever.

All the noble lines of the poets
did not make Hiroshima and Belsen
not to happen,
nor will they keep back the coming holocaust.

Why should you add
to the mischief,
the self-deception?
Leave that to the culture-peddlers.

Be truthful:
tell children who their forbears were,
the curse they bear.

Do not weaken
even a single one of them
with fine sentiments!

•

Le Tombeau de la Mort

While female poets
embroider (for the howmanyth time?)
on the theme of death
(lady, you dropped a stitch!)
and a fussy translator
presents their doilies
to the United Nations
in nine different languages,
I am concerned with the problems
of massculture.

I'm on the wharf reading a book
about Auschwitz.
Some lug is revving
his motorboat
up and down the lake,
enjoying the noise
and my discomfiture.

●

If he drowned
under the waves he makes
would the surrounding hills
miss him? the lake?
or I?
or even his family?

I do not think so.

So let us have no more death poems.
In this age of massmen
and mass deaths
they sound . . . they sound . . .
—well, just godawful!

•

Man Going Up and Down

Only he and I were in the lift.

"Do you like what you're doing?" I asked.

The lustreless stare he gave me was
One I've seen on coons crushed but intact
Lying inert on countryside roads;
But his voice burst like a tire: "I don't!"

"Then why not walk out with me—right now?"
We had reached my floor. "I'd desolate
This whole city, yes, massacre each
Man, woman, and child in it before
I'd let them put me into a cage
To run like a monkey up and down.
Come, leave behind you this accursed car.
Let it stand void for all eternity."

He now looked at me mistrustfully
As he opened the door. "Look, mister,"
He said, "You must be one of them men
I hear about with sharp ideas
For changing people's lives and the world.
I've been taught about the likes of you.
Well, no one is changing me, no sir.
I've my job and I'll stick to it, see?"

•

Not more proud looked young Alexander
In his tent among his Greek captains
The night he overwhelmed Darius,
Or blond Charles when he slew the Polacks,
Or Don Juan after his hundredth lay.

"You sad mutt," I said almost aloud
As he held up his head, offended.
I'd have thrown him a bone had I one.
"Civilization could not endure
A single hour without your trapped soul."
In the next instant he had changed back
Into the affable tool he was.

I strode out of the elevator.
A rush of stale air followed me out
And turning to find what had made it
I saw myself pursued by the shades
Of half-a-score indignant teachers,
Three pallid clergymen dressed in black,
And a vile woman, doubtless his wife
—Or the Medusa, if you prefer myths.

•

Lilith

I would for beauty of face
Unpeople Persia and Greece;
Kiss any old murderer
Who'll quench my body's furor
Though his victims' bones should crawl
Up to my own gate and wall.
Let the balladeers complain
Until their runes split in twain;
And timid sages despair
That blood and lust fill the air,
And virtuous folk bewail
When I scratch them with my nail:
Yet what do I have life for—
Or must I hear burghers snore?
The great Masters alone knew
All a woman's mind could do
And gave her, to have her wish,
No more conscience than a fish.
Ah, men, before you were dead

•

I'd enjoy you all in bed;
Then, having tasted my thighs,
You'd die off like poisoned flies;
Or having touched my quick once,
Perish in flames like red ants.
Give me the hero who'll strike
Heads off to put on a pike;
A Samson with bone of ass
To kill the unfevered mass,
The clods and lumps who yet thrive
Like cold graveworms near a grave.
Where is my remorseless lord
With blood smoking on his sword
And his head like a ship's prow?
Come, my Sun God, come, come now!
Your loins melt me, I desire
You drill my body with fire
For I burn with love and feel
Myself flame from head to heel.

•

The Sparks Fly

1. I go about making trouble for myself.
   The sparks fly.
   I gather each one
   and start a poem.

2. On the waxed twine
   of her affection
   her mouth goes up & down
   like a yo-yo.

3. Wives, womenfriends—something in me
   will not let them rest.
   What a queer universe this is
   when it takes three marriages
   to produce a seasoned poet.

4. She was pregnant
   and spoke of air-currents
   in her chest.
   When I bent down to kiss her
   she made a rude noise
   and smiled.
   What would Tennyson make of this?
   Or that idiot, Eliot?

5. The school where I teach
   is the bran pan
   of civilization;
   for kicks, I sometimes speak
   the lines of a poet
   to the caged astonished dimwits
   then wait for the gibbonous screech.

●

6. The smell of a religious
   woman
   past her menopause:
   No star, I'm sure,
   ever smelled like this,
   No living flower.

7. Why can't I let them die
   in their swamps,
   the sunless presbyterians of this country,
   peacefully, peacefully
   —not stir them up with my stick or pole?
   Phew! What a stink arises.
   What fetid, multi-coloured insects
   strike my head.

8. And the orgasmless women of Hampstead, why
   must I always press them
   to abandon their husbands and unsatisfactory
   lovers,
   or their deplorable tastes in literature?

9. She thinks if she labels
   the poison "love,"
   it will not disorder my blood
   or make my hair and teeth
   fall out.
   The bitch! whom does she think
   she's kidding?

•

10. Their everyday politics
    is diseased sex;
    had they a trifle more health
    they'd vote for an early death.

11. I heard three shit-birds
    in council whistle and chirk,
    while a castrato stood before them
    shaped like a tuning fork.

12. Ah, the dung-beetles that want my blood.
    Age and possessions have turned me into stone.
    There's no blood in a stone.
    Bang!
    Out of their crushed limbs
    I also make poems.

●

Portrait of an English Prof

A critic, he measures the erections
of famous writers
(English and continental)

having no use for native talent
in poetry or prose,
scanning these with a critical eye
borrowed from Mr Leavis

and is especially witty
at ladies' teas
about their perversions,
speaking in a high-pitched voice

and he has of course
an unfinished masterpiece
in his drawers
which he will show no one

not even his wife
for fear, he would have us think,
somebody might take it
out of his hands

Lord, keep me from puking
Lord, keep me from puking
Lord, keep me from puking

●

The Bishopric

Yes, and finding my small friar
sullen, cowled and scowling
in his beggar's posture:

Ha, my voice went sour
for the college girl squirming
under my length of form.
"I must reread my own poems,"
I said bitterly. "Or so it seems."

"Luckily for you," she breathed,
"no one will ever believe this
—not even your worst biographer."

I roared and that did it.
There was an instant election
as she brought her youthful face,
laughing,
into the sweet diocese of my body.

•

Sutra

It is hard to keep the mind
evenly balanced,
said the Buddha.

But that is not so;
my mind
is evenly balanced
on the two buttock cheeks
of my beloved.

And poised perfectly
on what is around
and below.

•

To a Lily
for A. J. M. Smith

Smith, you're no poet but an onion;
For seeing your shrivelled head all but done
You plant it in mine or Dudek's compost:
Shout when up shoots a green little riposte.

And I shout with you, only amazed
That you should look astonished and so dazed;
'Twasn't the head made the stem rise and curl—
Think of the soil, dear Art, the manured soil!

If dying lilies smell worse than weeds,
Your ruptured bulbs, decaying, nurture reeds;
May—who can tell?—redeem the years' sad waste
With smallish onions pungent to the taste.

Yet struck was I, as was the world, when
To serve the Commonwealth, a courtly Pan,
Upon a single onion shoot you blew
A whole fierce verse from start to finish through.

•

Twittering of loves safe and loyal,
Of ties not republican but royal;
God, how square can a captured faun get
Who wants still other poems to Margaret?

Leave off, my wan professor, leave off;
Those Arnold and Hopkins wrote are enough.
I write for no child and for no mermaid;
My artless ambition is to get laid

In the loveliest cunts I know
Lest I also through onion reeds shall blow
False Loyalist sentiment one black day,
Out of sight, sightless, in the U.S.A.

•

Lazarus

He thinks because he once
tried to shoot himself
and failed
he now understands
everything about life.

Who will tell this Lazarus
in the pin-striped suit
that he smells of the grave
and that I've seen worms
stand up in his eyes and mouth?

•

Make Mine Vodka

Change

There may be, comrades,
as you say, no God;
but there is death.
And the grass,
no matter what's buried
under it
comes up smelling fresh and sweet.

Mysteries

Comrade Mikoyan,
why do you go on living?

Flower in a crannied wall . . .
but if I knew
why Comrade Mikoyan
wishes to go on living
(and goes on living)
I would understand
me, and thee, and all.

The Wave of the Future

The East Germans
are not running away
from Communism;
they're just coming
to tell us,
somewhat breathlessly,
how wonderful it all is.

•

Russian Intellectual & Collective Leadership

Now that the great Stalin is dead and gone,
He has five holes to smell instead of one.

Red Square

Evgeny Evtushenko,
fable-maker
and world-famous successor
to Pushkin, finds
angry young men
a phenomenon of the West.
COMRADES: bourgeois skin inflammations!

His own country
being declared perfect,
no one with eyes to see
would ever think to complain
—certainly no Russ poet,
great lover of life & freedom.

•

Epigram for Roy Daniells

Wise men for stys think him fit
And thinking on it will spit;
And colleagues though tamed they be
Find none so gelded as he:
A professorial ox
To be stalled in a close box.
Some would hold him in a ditch
—His very breath causes itch!
And those whom he gave the mange
Would loose him on a wide range.
I, to my immortal den
Bring this unsavoury man:
I, for now and for all times
Toss this Daniells to the lines.

•

Whom I Write For

When reading me, I want you to feel
   as if I had ripped your skin off;
Or gouged out your eyes with my fingers;
Or scalped you, and afterwards burnt your hair
   in the staring sockets; having first filled them
with fluid from your son's lighter.
I want you to feel as if I had slammed
   your child's head against a spike;
And cut off your member and stuck it in your
   wife's mouth to smoke like a cigar.

For I do not write to improve your soul;
   or to make you feel better, or more humane;
Nor do I write to give you new emotions;
Or to make you proud to be able to experience them
   or to recognize them in others.
I leave that to the fraternity of lying poets
   —no prophets, but toadies and trained seals!
How much evil there is in the best of them
   as their envy and impotence flower into poems
And their anality into love of man, into virtue:
Especially when they tell you, sensitively,
   what it feels like to be a potato.

•

I write for the young man, demented,
    who dropped the bomb on Hiroshima;
I write for Nasser and Ben Gurion;
For Krushchev and President Kennedy;
    for the Defence Secretary
voted forty-six billions for the extirpation
    of humans everywhere.
I write for the Polish officers machine-gunned
    in the Katyn forest;
I write for the gassed, burnt, tortured,
    and humiliated everywhere;
I write for Castro and tse-Tung, the only poets
    I ever learned anything from;
I write for Adolph Eichmann, compliant clerk
    to that madman, the human race;
For his devoted wife and loyal son.

Give me words fierce and jagged enough
    to tear your skin like shrapnel;
Hot and searing enough to fuse
    the flesh off your blackened skeleton;
Words with the sound of crunching bones or bursting eyeballs;
    or a nose being smashed with a gun butt;
Words with the soft plash of intestines
    falling out of your belly;
Or cruel and sad as the thought which tells you "This is the end"
And you feel Time oozing out of your veins
    and yourself becoming one with the weightless dark.

•

A Harsh Karsh

Looselips

A cross is our Prime Minister
Between a rabbit and a rooster:
For when he speaks about policy
Loose lips and teeth nibble celery
At the same time that he shakes
His fat wattles in the wind he makes.

The Obstruction

A cold potato from chin to crown,
He speaks with an obstruction in his throat
His bowtie holds and won't let down.

And he's too well-bred to touch his mouth
Though the hand he waggles with such a frown
Itches to yank the damn thing out!

•

Stranger in Town

Spinous and indignant,
She told the lace merchant:
"People are that crooked,
O the world is that wicked
I've had my rosary
Stolen—and in church too!
It was taken today
From my very own pew.
If I should find the thief
I'd hack both his hands off."

I heard the merchant say:
"It happens every day.
Father O'Keefe warns us
Not to leave our bibles;
But these and missals bring
When we come after Mass
Or missals will be missing,
The bibles gone, alas.
Our town is a queer place,"
Said the merchant of lace.

I thought, for all he sighed,
His voice was tinged with pride.

•

Poem for the Peerless Queen

I was alone in the field.

Thirstily I drank
all the beer I had brought,
emptying the vacuum flask
in two swallows.

I rose afterwards
and with poor aim
cooled off
the egocentric bee
mauling a flower cluster.

All the wet leaves around
glistened; and one,
having trapped the sun,
sparkled like a crown jewel
in the field
of monotonous green:

Became, stirred
by the wind,
a tongue of white laughter
in the mouth of the valley.

But I doubt
if I can get
the peerless queen
to go for that.

·

On a Clothing Manufacturer

Nowadays a malook if he's got the kale
Gets his ass kissed uncommonly clean;
All tongues are his, this fart from a latrine.
Fart? Flea in the straw of some stinking jail.
Why I, Irving Layton, know such a one
Right here in this city—a manufacturer
Of suits—whose dam, a sharp trader in whores,
Gave him his taste for holes and buttons.
Boy, you ought to see how the Directors
Sidle up to him, all smiles; how they itch
To get that first lick in, each son-of-a-bitch
Of them—cultured men, too, doctors, lawyers:
While I, if he turned to me his prickface,
Would let go on it, friends, from a high place.

At Desjardins

He: executive suite,
a moneyed lout;
she: a middle-aged harpy,
a hunk of powdered
and perfumed meat,
waiting for him
to clean his plate
and drop dead.

What amorous,
open-eyed poet
could be bothered
cursing them?
Look at them.
When all is said,
aren't they cursed
enough, my friends,
as is?

But the waitress
by their silence
knows the poisoned
meat they eat,
and with practised grin

Gives each a glass
of clear water;
and removing the dishes,
her good wishes
for a quick digestion.

•

Gifts

I left two dollars for a taxi.
I did it discreetly.
I placed the money on a chair,
Knowing she would find it there.

The next day my darling flew at me.
"You hurt me terribly.
Gifts: as many as you please
But not . . ." I stroked her knees

And waited. "Who'd be upset,"
She sobbed, "by a bracelet?
Or even dismayed
By earrings, pearl-inlaid?

"An alluring perfume,
Or some small thing for my room,
A vase or silver dish?
Gifts: as many as you wish.

"But not, mon chèr, money.
That dishonours both you and me."
In Cosette's swimming eyes
I could see the fleshly compromise:

Where sharpest knife won't cut
Wounded honour from appetite,
And self with the first kiss
Turns love into a casuist.

•

Supernatural Event at Cedar Pond

"The flowers," I said, "in the hollow where we lie
Take sun and moon with a fine natural aplomb;
Don't whine, never hold up their cold extremities
As a reproach to the State of New Hampshire
Or look as if their fate was anyone's concern
—Not even my own, my fretting pet;
And certainly not that of the cosmos."
I was about to say more when Dorothy Wordsworth
I discerned, a bright look in her mad eyes,
And Emily running free across the heath.

I saw them, I aver, up there ahead of me
On that not-too-distant, fragrant hill,
Turning their visionary heads to glance back, shy,
As if to say, "Walk here between us, if you will."
And I would too, you know, for women ghosts
Who love the hills and clouds, rain and mist,
The purple look on mountain and sky,
Wind and late evening birdcall
Hold for me no supernatural dread at all
—Far less than young wives that fret all day and squall.

Yet all I said was: "Come here, poor devil,
And let me kiss your damp fingers
More limp than last week's cut celery;
Perhaps my lips will suck up their frost,
Dispel the conspiracies of cloud
That've kept you hovering over the fire, a sad
And shivering bride: the bad weather scramble finally
Over the famous beechtrees and get lost,
And the ragged curtains of mist for your sake
Lift from this region and this rented lake."

•

She was silent. I said, "My Strange One, hear me:
That very night before we met and wed
I walked into an expected storm
And though later the winds shook the trees and me
And the skies bled, I sang like an Italian tenor
Into the wild, electric darkness for an hour
While all about me enormous flashbulbs went off.
Someone up there was taking the picture,
Front views and profiles, of a solitary happy man
—You may scoff—was snapping it again and again.

"My Love, they say God himself asks to see
These photographs from time to time;
It must give him a most heavenly lift
To know someone like me walks the earth,
A single ecstatic man on his planet.
(Imagine me with face and hair all wet,
My mouth open, and one soaking foot
Thrust out defiantly before the other!)
Yet now that I consider it, I wonder
At the antique photography that still needs thunder!"

Her face grew more unsmiling; I saw her frown
And felt as when clouds suddenly darken
And a chilling wind blows on heated limbs.
So to humour her, lift my own unease, I laughed:
"Perhaps when Lucifer visits heaven again,
The Almighty flourishing a snapshot of me
Will say, 'Forget poor Job, dear Satan,
See if you can topple *him*, this joyous one.'"
My darling's eyes grew green as moss, then baleful red.
Her hands furred, I swooned and was left here for dead.

•

The Dazed Steer

for Norman Mailer

He greeted me by saying:
"What if I hit you in the belly?"

We squared off
and stared at each other's eyes
for a full minute.
"You're the first draw
I've had this evening, man,"
he said, then turned his head
like a dazed steer.

And I knew that someone or something
had dealt him a blow
from which he'd never recover.

•

Agnus Dei

Ah, the Catholic genius.

At the Oratoire St Joseph,
on display, Brother André's
discoloured, miracle-working truss.

And here
in a quiet grove
away from the cottages
crowding the lake
and the summer noises,
a rustic shrine
to the Mother of Love
—an old bathtub
one end sawed off
and painted white and green.

O blessed vision!
The transfiguring
of common things;
the holifying
of even the mean.

Still, little mother,
I do not use a truss;
and prefer
to the most satisfactory
of baths,
cold showers.

•

Questions

Why is it
that when a man says
he's a realist,
his mouth, his eyes
at once
become fierce and ugly
and he looks
as if he's about
to wipe out
your whole family?
And why is it
when a woman says,
"I love you"
her mouth begins
to work curiously
as if she was getting ready
for a meal?
And why haven't the poets
made more
of the fact
that man is the only animal
who sings
and has haemorrhoids?

•

Five Women

I

You are grass.
You are earth and water.
You are sunlight on a rock.

Out of the burning air
you place your lace panties
on my hidden altar.
What a queer incense now arises!
The lighted tapers snicker.

Like sands thrown at a ruined door
your lips scrape at my ear:
"Love sees better in the dark."
Your mouth blows out the dying taper
and I fall down on the sunlit grass
and hold your perfect breasts like water.

II

The mother of seven children,
six daughters and a grown-up son,
she still finds sex distasteful
and walks like a somnambulist,
unawakened and virginal,
saying, "Whose children are these?
Where do I come from from?"

Sex is beautiful as the earth.
In her it has crumbled into dirt.

•

III

I love water.
Not this thin drizzle of pleasure.

IV

The earth is beautiful.
The grass is beautiful.
But she covers them both
with a picnic tablecloth
and sets wines and comestibles before me.
Before making love, she says,
one should eat well,
being careful of the digestion.

Seeing the sausage grease
on her honest hands and neck,
I half expect to find love
explained in a cook book.

V

I love earth.
I love grass.
I love water.
I love the sun,
and death
as final consummation.

•

But a sexless woman is not death;
is the odour of death,
of cerements and coffin wood.

Why doesn't this unlovely woman die,
instead of uselessly brushing her teeth
and polishing her fingernails?
When she smiles I see bits of cerement-cloth
between her teeth;
when she bends her fleshless arm
it is as if a coffin lid came softly down.

•

Love Among the Cannibals

Having enjoyed
his delectable piece
from Hampstead
he waited for the tender aftermath.

It came with the coffee and cigarettes.

"I wonder how hairy Harry
would perform in bed,"
she smiled. "Or Stanley.
I've always—since a child—
been curious about men
with small feet and big hands."

In silence
he reached for the tableknife
and stared at his short, stubby fingers
twitching to stroke her neck.

"Want these for sugar lumps?"
he grinned back.

·

Merlin Perverse

What do you want, my silly Aviva?
For the splendid sun to shine each day?
Or for me to paste one in the sky
And order the clouds to keep away?

You hold up your frozen fingertips
And blow on them and curse;
As if the blood level in them
Disclosed earth's goodness or reverse.

Get angry at black skies, my pet;
Rave of Haiti and Mexico;
I'll split the ground beneath your feet
And warm your cold bones below.

•

Friends

S—— loves you, I said.
She'd do anything to help you.

Yes, my woman replied,
she'd stand at my bedside
if I had a hysterectomy
or both legs were amputated;
and put herself into hock
if my eyes needed removal
because of cancer.

Well, tell her I'd do the same for her.

•

Who's Crazy?

When I was warm-hearted,
impulsive;
and would've given the skin
off my back
and gone to hell
for any one of them,
people ran from me
as from a leper,
my cries of love
the leper's warning bell.

Now I've become stone
and don't bat an eyelash
if someone is lashed
or ripped apart
before my eyes,
everyone says I'm serene
—Olympian!—
and cannot praise me enough
for my maturity.

And what I want to know is:
Who's crazy?
They? Or I?

•

The Gods Speak Out

Yes, yes. Sarajevo or Berlin:
That's our name for doing mankind in.

Men we loathe; women, only less so.
Into the holocaust let them go.

Yet on these creatures, malign, perverse,
Is laid no irremediable curse.

Untimely made out of air and slime,
Disorder hurtles them into crime.

For reason and conscience, subtle pair,
Engendered by the luminous air

When streaked with mud that nothing may cleanse
Are both perverted, serve evil ends.

Their reason into simple cunning grows
To first invent, then destroy, their foes.

•

While conscience leads them to devise
Foul delusions and hypocrisies.

And those whom reason and conscience maim,
The pale companions of guilt and shame:

The virtuous who dam up their hell,
The meek—why, we know these by their smell!

And there's not one whom power to kill
Does not secretly exalt and thrill.

Ah, plagued by light as by the dark, men
Must hurt their kind however they can.

Harder it is to love than to hate;
More thrilling to ruin than to create.
We do nothing; merely watch and wait.

•

The Hag

I, though fifty years, am defenceless.
The white hairs of my beard fool no one.
I make a face, but even the crones laugh.

The absurd laugh reaching an inn,
Five men begin talking at once.
They embrace and call each other friends.

Farmers, workers, rise from the ground
Like vapour: hands covered with hammers;
Between their fierce grinning lips, needles

To pierce my eyeballs. So housewives,
Shredding onions, will clench a burnt
Matchstick with their lips to hold back tears.

I'm a monstrosity ripped
Out of the night, and my first rattle
Was a tree and a shivering toad.

•

Fire claimed me at birth, and a hag
Waits to puncture the jagged red scar
Under my chin that sealed our compact.

When I proved she was an angel
She bit her own vein and died, who now
Presses me to limn her dark portrait

Even here in this timeless square,
Before this gay, good-natured crowd
Idly appraising the needle's point.

I've seen a dead Algerian child;
And a crushed grass-snake curse the sun,
And a defenceless hare on the heath

Pray to the moon to sheathe its light,
Its terrible and beautiful light.
Farmers, workers, and all good people:

My eyes are open; I am waiting.

●

Ambiguities of Conduct

He was telling me
how important love was,
lamenting the atrophy
of human emotion
in our mechanical age.

It was apparent
he was well up
in Lawrence and Kierkegaard;
moreover, the man was sincere.

Even if, later,
he deliberately flicked
his cigarette ash
into a flowercup
where a black insect
was crawling.

But neither the sizzle
nor the scream
(which I alone heard)
interrupted his excited
words of love.

The Divine Madman

He seized me by the throat and shouted:
"Admit there's no love in each of us;
Man hates his kind and wishes him ill,
And there's no God and there never was!
And in this indifferent universe
Our virtue's to make one vermin less—
Without love, this life is mean and cold:
I curse it!" And he tightened his hold.
And had I not gasped I loved Man well,
My poor end was simple to foretell.

•

The Architect

I put my hand through a hedge;
   the leaves of the roadside shrubbery stirred,
scattering immense grains of countryside dust.

The forest behind me began to sneeze,
   and blew into the quiet noon air
thrushes, sparrows, and red-winged cardinals.

They fell at my feet like coloured snowflakes;
   from their tiny, beautiful bones
I raised a city where the first bird had fallen.

The mayor's wife, resembling Alice B. Toklas,
   donated her most attractive smile
to decorate the flagpole of the tallest building.

On clear nights even dwarfs can see her dentures
   outlined against the sky as if
to snap at the moon or a moon man descending.

From a nearby swamp I came to another forest
   while humming the first faint banknotes
that came into my head and thinking of means

•

To squeeze the silver from the moon and stars.
    When I put my hand through a hedge
the forest just held its breath and gulped.

No bird dropped. A toad suddenly leaped up
    and looked me straight in the eye;
he remained suspended in mid air until he fell.

Yet when I pulled back my eager hand
    my wrist was thick as a porcupine
and ugly with huge unshaven bristles.

The toothless wife of the mayor, however,
    will not let me amputate:
my queer arm, she says, is a civic acquisition.

Together when we walk arm-in-arm on Sherbrooke St.
    we make an intriguing pair;
tourists of all countries just stand and stare.

•

Breakdown

I knew him for a cultivated
gentleman,
a lover of operas
and a Latinist
who had annotated the De Amicitia
to the acclaim of scholars.

We were in Parc Lafontaine,
admiring the instinctual swans.
There was nothing in his behaviour
—in his walk or talk—
to make me suspicious.

As we passed
the blind woman sitting alone
on one of the benches,
he stopped suddenly before her
and plunged two pins,
one into each cheek.

●

I heard the blind woman's
terrified shrieks
as he said quietly:
"I can't understand her rage;
my ancestors would have pierced her
with javelins.
She ought to be grateful
we live in a reasonable age."

Of course they put him into the loony bin
where he shares a cell
with a distinguished anthropologist
and one other Latinist.

·

Advice for Two Young Poets

The idea's to drive *them* to madness and drink
—not yourselves;
or to suicide.
Consider well the lives of Crane and Poe
and that magnificent slob, Mayakovsky,
who played Russian roulette
with his genius:
then go and do otherwise!
Theirs is not the way. No. No.
In Apollo's name, don't panic.
Why? What for?
You have the choicest weapons—words;
and *their* wives and daughters
will always be yours for the taking.
Learn from Boris, a fox if ever there was one,
outliving Stalin and the other brutes.
That's it, that's the main thing, survival.
And do not be overfinicky here: steal
if you must; kill
if there's no help for it.
One miserable human more or less hardly matters
but the loss of a good poem does,
being irreplaceable.
God knows how many corpses
I have rotting neatly in my cellar.
I gave up counting long ago.

●

The Fool's Song

When I look back upon my life,
   What do I find?
   What do I find?
A single star, when I was seven,
That lit up earth and heaven;
   And here and there
   Some few wise and fair
But most, alas, unkind, unkind.

When I look back upon my days,
   What do I see?
   What do I see?
A thrush that sang from a windowsill,
Soul and ears to have their fill;
   But neighbours cried
   And my joy denied
And scared that bird, that bird, from me.

When I look back but yesterday—
   Ah, what befell?
   Ah, what befell?
A woman I told of bird and star,
Gleams and sounds that come from far;
   She brought me here
   Without sigh or tear
And bid me sing, but sing of hell.

•

If I Lie Still

If I lie still
the light from the leaves
will drop on my hands and knees

Fire will envelop me
yet I won't burn

I shall hear the silence plainly
while the stream flows into my veins
and out again

Small wild animals will no longer fear me,
but bring their young
to tickle my heels,
nuzzle in my armpits

I shall know love without disquiet
—without passion

For a thousand years
I shall lie like this
with my head toward the sun

Till knowledge and power
have become one;
then I shall write a single verse,
achieve one flawless deed

Then lie down again
to become like this shallow
stone under my hand,
and let my face
be covered with grass

To be pulled out by the roots
by what raging hermit,
his breast torn apart as mine now?

•

What Does It Matter?

This has been a rainy summer.
Once or twice we quarrelled.
What does it matter?
The main thing as we say
when we embrace
is that we love each other:
that, mutatis mutandis, we know
with the finality of calendar
and equinox
the summer's here
though the days are sullen and wet
and our teeth shake at night
louder than wooden windowframes.

Yes, I have known loose garrulous women.
What does it matter?
And restless, beautiful ones
that intoxicated me with flattery and drink.
What does it matter?
And sad helpless ones
that reached out for love
no one nowadays gives
and the pinheads sneer at and besmirch.
Again, what does it matter?
A poet lives in a special hell
—it has a view opening on heaven;
and whether it is disgust, hatred of death,
concupiscence, love, or aspiration
that broils and blisters him here
not even the Devil can tell
though he's seen many queer ones in his time.

•

The price comes high
for the kind of immortality I want;
still, I am shamed by your greatness,
your savage pertinacity.
You have earned your own coign in hell,
with me (what a crazy paradox!)
your small glimpse of heaven.
So be it.
There have been other strange pairs in history;
and anyway what's this life for
if not to proliferate conundrum and mystery
for the journalists to be amazed at?

Yet believe this:
it is my destiny
from any ditch
to walk out clean;
and though I lie drunk with poetry and wine,
my back is never to the stars,
my face never in the muck;
and always I feel your presence
brooding over me like the summer sky
where your face, a star,
is clearly seen
(Ah, I am really sloshed!)
and multiplied in the million lights that shine.

Butterfly on Rock

The large yellow wings, black-fringed,
were motionless

They say the soul of a dead person
will settle like that on the still face

But I thought: the rock has borne this;
this butterfly is the rock's grace,
its most obstinate and secret desire
to be a thing alive made manifest

Forgot were the two shattered porcupines
I had seen die in the bleak forest.
Pain is unreal; death, an illusion:
There is no death in all the land,
I heard my voice cry;
And brought my hand down on the butterfly
And felt the rock move beneath my hand.

A Tall Man Executes a Jig
for Malcolm Ross

I

So the man spread his blanket on the field
And watched the shafts of light between the tufts
And felt the sun push the grass towards him;
The noise he heard was that of whizzing flies,
The whistlings of some small imprudent birds,
And the ambiguous rumbles of cars
That made him look up at the sky, aware
Of the gnats that tilted against the wind
And in the sunlight turned to jigging motes.
Fruitflies he'd call them except there was no fruit
About, spoiling to hatch these glitterings,
These nervous dots for which the mind supplied
The closing sentences from Thucydides,
Or from Euclid having a savage nightmare.

II

Jig jig, jig jig. Like minuscule black links
Of a chain played with by some playful
Unapparent hand or the palpitant
Summer haze bored with the hour's stillness.
He felt the sting and tingle afterwards
Of those leaving their orthodox unrest,
Leaving their undulant excitation
To drop upon his sleeveless arm. The grass,
Even the wildflowers became black hairs
And himself a maddened speck among them.
Still the assaults of the small flies made him
Glad at last, until he saw purest joy
In their frantic jiggings under a hair,
So changed from those in the unrestraining air.

•

III

He stood up and felt himself enormous.
Felt as might Donatello over stone,
Or Plato, or as a man who has held
A loved and lovely woman in his arms
And feels his forehead touch the emptied sky
Where all antinomies flood into light.
Yet jig jig jig, the haloing black jots
Meshed with the wheeling fire of the sun:
Motion without meaning, disquietude
Without sense or purpose, ephemerides
That mottled the resting summer air till
Gusts swept them from his sight like wisps of smoke.
Yet they returned, bringing a bee who, seeing
But a tall man, left him for a marigold.

IV

He doffed his aureole of gnats and moved
Out of the field as the sun sank down,
A dying god upon the blood-red hills.
Ambition, pride, the ecstasy of sex,
And all circumstance of delight and grief,
That blood upon the mountain's side, that flood
Washed into a clear incredible pool
Below the ruddied peaks that pierced the sun.
He stood still and waited. If ever
The hour of revelation was come
It was now, here on the transfigured steep.
The sky darkened. Some birds chirped. Nothing else.
He thought the dying god had gone to sleep:
An Indian fakir on his mat of nails.

●

V

And on the summit of the asphalt road
Which stretched towards the fiery town, the man
Saw one hill raised like a hairy arm, dark
With pines and cedars against the stricken sun
—The arm of Moses or of Joshua.
He dropped his head and let fall the halo
Of mountains, purpling and silent as time,
To see temptation coiled before his feet:
A violated grass snake that lugged
Its intestine like a small red valise.
A cold-eyed skinflint it now was, and not
The manifest of that joyful wisdom,
The mirth and arrogant green flame of life;
Or earth's vivid tongue that flicked in praise of earth.

VI

And the man wept because pity was useless.
"Your jig's up; the flies come like kites," he said
And watched the grass snake crawl towards the hedge,
Convulsing and dragging into the dark
The satchel filled with curses for the earth,
For the odours of warm sedge, and the sun,
A blood-red organ in the dying sky.
Backwards it fell into a grassy ditch
Exposing its underside, white as milk,
And mocked by wisps of hay between its jaws;
And then it stiffened to its final length.
But though it opened its thin mouth to scream
A last silent scream that shook the black sky,
Adamant and fierce, the tall man did not curse.

•

VII

Beside the rigid snake the man stretched out
In fellowship of death; he lay silent
And stiff in the heavy grass with eyes shut,
Inhaling the moist odours of the night
Through which his mind tunnelled with flicking tongue
Backwards to caves, mounds, and sunken ledges
And desolate cliffs where come only kites,
And where of perished badgers and racoons
The claws alone remain, gripping the earth.
Meanwhile the green snake crept upon the sky,
Huge, his mailed coat glittering with stars that made
The night bright, and blowing thin wreaths of cloud
Athwart the moon; and as the weary man
Stoop up, coiled above his head, transforming all.

•

Acknowledgements

I wish to thank the editors of the following
periodicals for permission to reprint poems they
originally published: *The Canadian Forum, Queen's
Quarterly, The Tamarack Review, Evidence, Cata-
ract, Exchange, The Outsider,* and *The Fiddlehead.*
I also wish to thank my friends, Mr and Mrs
William Goodwin, for impatiently enduring for two
whole summers the irascibility of my genius. And
all lovers of poetry are indebted with me to Mr
and Mrs Carl Katz, who by unravelling for me the
mysteries of real estate investment, not only allowed
me to understand the financial aspect of Shakes-
peare's genius, but did more for poetry in the long
run than all the universities, culture-peddlers, English profs, and poetry-promoters lumped together.

•

•

·

•

•

•

THE AUTHOR

&

THE BOOK

In a recent survey of Canadian poetry, Milton Wilson said of Irving Layton:

"I look forward to elaborate and fantastic visions of judgement, to wry, subtle, even comic exploitations of his aging ego, and finally to the full poetic emergence of Layton the moralist and dramatist."

In *Balls for a One-Armed Juggler*, Layton has fufilled these predictions made by one of Canada's most perceptive and intelligent critics. This is a book to put beside Whitman's *Leaves of Grass* and Baudelaire's *Flowers of Evil* as achieving an intense personal definition.

Layton asks in his Foreword: "What insight does the modern poet give us into the absolute evil of our time?" He believes the poet must remember "he addresses mankind at large, not small coteries of the frightened and sensitive" and that "there is a new dark knowledge waiting to be assimilated into the minds and consciences of those who are his contemporaries."

This volume is a distillation of Layton's previous ones. The same preoccupations are here—poetry, sex, society, evil—but they have been crystallized by an enlarged and more complex awareness as well as by a severe mastery of craft so that only the purest elements remain.

Regarded by many as this country's most substantial poet, Irving Layton has published sixteen volumes of original work, besides editing two anthologies of Canadian verse, the most recent of which is the very successful *Love Where the Nights Are Long*. His poems have appeared in numerous Canadian, American, and English periodicals and have been translated into Italian, Spanish, Portuguese, German, and French. In 1960 he received the Governor-General's Medal for his *A Red Carpet for the Sun* and in the following year the President's Medal from the University of Western Ontario. He won a Canada Council award in 1959.

THE PUBLISHERS